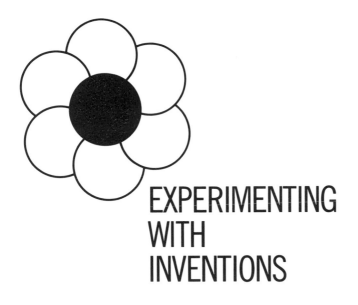

EXPERIMENTING WITH INVENTIONS

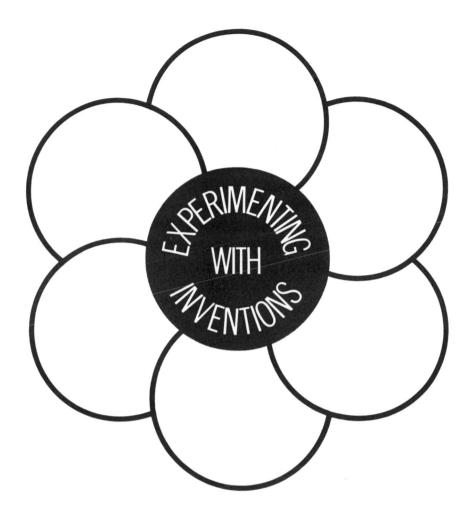

EXPERIMENTING WITH INVENTIONS

BY ROBERT GARDNER

FRANKLIN WATTS 1990
NEW YORK LONDON TORONTO SYDNEY
A VENTURE BOOK

All photos courtesy of Robert Gardner, except:
New York Public Library, Picture Collection: **pp.** 40, **41**.

Library of Congress Cataloging-in-Publication Data

Gardner, Robert, 1929–
    Experimenting with inventions / by Robert Gardner.
        p.   cm.—(A Venture book)
    Includes bibliographical references.
    Summary: Discusses how common household items can
become useful inventions, how many inventions were discovered accidentally, and how new products can be patented.
    ISBN: 0-531-10910-0
    1. Inventions—Juvenile literature.   [1. Inventions.]
I. Title.
T48.G36   1990
609–dc20   89-24788   CIP   AC

A special thanks to the following people who allowed the author to photograph the old tools and other articles found in chapter 2:

James Bates
Alfred Conklin
Marjorie Menconi
Jesse Sanford
Mario Sebben

CONTENTS

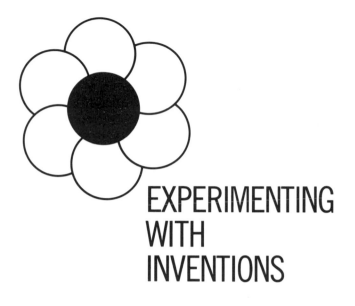

EXPERIMENTING
WITH
INVENTIONS

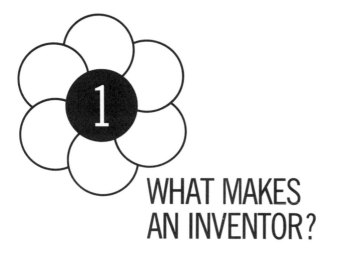

WHAT MAKES
AN INVENTOR?

Ralph Waldo Emerson, an early nineteenth-century American writer, is reported to have said, "Build a better mousetrap and the world will beat a path to your door."

A lot of people must have taken Emerson's words to heart. Since 1838 there have been 3,300 patents issued for mousetraps. However, despite the large number of patents, 150 years of ever-improving mousetraps have hardly made mice an endangered species.

The trap seen on page 12 is a recent one. The mouse, lured by cheese or peanut butter placed at the front of the trap,

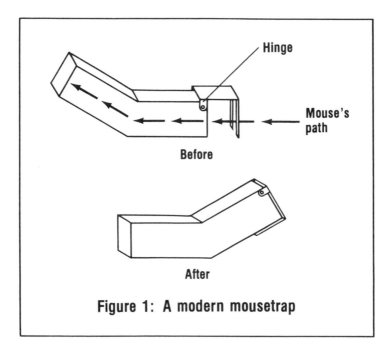

Before

After

Figure 1: A modern mousetrap

enters through the open end. As he walks toward the front end of the "tunnel," the trap tips forward. Because the mouse will not back up, he is trapped in the tunnel. Such a trap does not kill the mouse the way other traps do; captured mice may be returned to a world outside the house.

Mouse traps, like other inventions, are patented by the Patent and Trademark Office (PTO), a division of the U.S. Commerce Department. If you invent a new mouse-trap and receive a patent for it, you will have a seventeen-year monopoly on that invention. It was the PTO that issued Thomas Edison a patent for his electric light in 1879.

WHAT INVENTORS SAY • According to Ben du Pont, a young man who works as an inventor for a large corporation and also as an independent inventor, the best inventors are good at generating quality ideas in great quantity. A good inventor must be able to produce many potential solutions to a problem. Further, he or she must be able to choose the best idea for solving a problem and pursue it with determination until it works.

"Ideas," says du Pont, "are not thought of in neat logical order. They surface amid chaos and confusion. Our society and schooling repress this fact and try to convince us that ideas arise from logical thought processes. Nothing is farther from the truth."

Mr. du Pont, like most inventors, keeps a notebook in which he records ideas, data, results, and so on. He even keeps a small pad beside his bed because he sometimes wakes up in the night with a new thought or a possible solution to a problem that he has been thinking about. "Often," he says, "new ideas arise from failures. Something doesn't work, but by understanding why it didn't work you suddenly understand why something else *will* work."

There are two types of inventors, according to du Pont. The first are those with expertise in a particular technical field. These inventors have a good understanding of one area of knowledge and their inventions are generally limited to that area. The second are broad-based inventors who are able to bring together diverse technologies to produce something entirely new. The second type may have very little technical training; they may not even be well educated, though they do possess great insight and imagination. "But regardless of whether you are independent or work for a corporation," says du Pont, "as an inventor, you've got to be willing to stick your neck out, to take chances, to be different."

Unlike Thomas Edison, Samuel Morse, Charles Goodyear, and other independent inventors of the nineteenth century, today's inventors are less evident because most of them are employed by large corporations. Their patents are owned by the companies for whom they work. There are advantages to working for a large firm. You don't have to worry about finding someone to finance your work; you have lots of expensive equipment to work with; and you have other inventive and intelligent minds to offer helpful suggestions and criticism. On the other hand, often you have less freedom in choosing what you want to investigate.

"Brainstorming with others," says du Pont, "is very useful. The collision of ideas, even wild ones, can result in entirely new ideas. Strange and very different ideas sometimes come together in a novel way."

Sometimes an individual inventor will brainstorm alone, recording various ideas and looking among them for connections that provide new ideas or solutions to old problems. Such brainstorming led du Pont to invent "Gravity Bloxs," a novel educational toy for children.

Curtis Prince is another young inventor, an independent. He lives in Florida, and describes himself as an amateur physicist and self-taught mechanic. To provide the funds he needs to pursue his inventions and seek patents, Curtis works as an insurance agent. But he looks forward to the day when he can devote all his energies to inventing. And that day may not be far off!

Curtis, who used to participate in motorcross races, holds a patent for a device that allows the rear wheel of a motorcycle to "give" when it strikes a bump. But his latest patent, one for an all-terrain vehicle (ATV), has a greater potential for monetary reward.

The Consumer Product Safety Commission (CPSC) wants to ban the sale of ATV's in the United States. Eventually, all such vehicles may be recalled because each year they cause a number of deaths and injuries.

Prince, who is well aware of the dangers of ATV's, saw an opportunity to save lives *and* make money. In responding to this "hot idea," he invented the "Celestial Traverser" (CT), an ATV that is much safer than present models. The drawings on page 16, which were done by Prince, clearly show why the CT is a safer vehicle. It has a flexible frame that allows its wheels to rise independently over bumps without tipping the entire frame. On curves, the flexible frame allows the rider to bend inward like a cyclist.

A Japanese firm has already approached Prince about buying the patent rights to the Celestial Traverser. However, companies may fear that if they produce the CT, it will imply that their earlier models were badly engineered.

Whether or not his Celestial Traverser ever reaches the dealers' showrooms, Curtis Prince will go on inventing. It's in his blood, and he has many more ideas in his files and his mind. When asked how he thinks of new

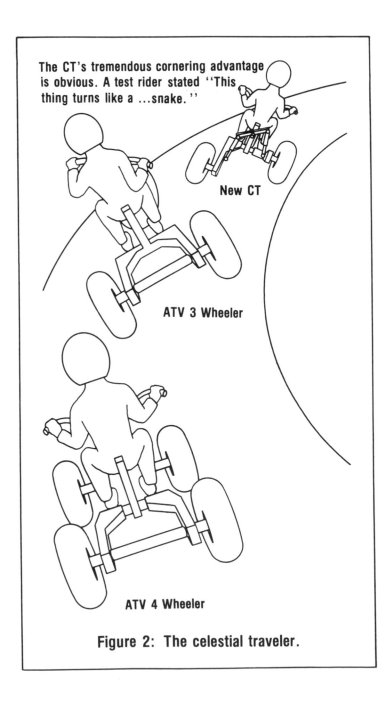

Figure 2: The celestial traveler.

ideas, he replied, "They just keep coming!" He went on to say that if he were interested in inventing a better kite, he'd spend a week or two just flying kites. He'd look for the factors that make a kite fly best.

Like so many inventors, Prince uses his intuition, experience, and a lot of hard thinking in arriving at his inventions.

COMMON CHARACTERISTICS OF INVENTORS • In his book, *Inventors at Work,* Kenneth A. Brown discusses his interviews with well known inventors. Their comments and responses to Brown's questions reinforce the statements of Ben du Pont and Curtis Prince regarding the process of inventing. In general, a quality commonly found among inventors is the ability to think laterally; that is, to find connections between unrelated ideas and things. Though inventors can and do think logically, it is usually after they have arrived at an idea. It is their ability to make associations between things normally seen as unrelated that characterizes inventors. It is this trait that is often the source of new ideas—ideas that just "pop out."

Inventors are curious about the world. They observe things that most people miss. They are constantly asking, "How does it work?" and "How could I make it work better?" Often serendipity, the finding of things not sought for, plays a role in their work. While probing one problem, they may find the answer to another that they had put aside. Paul MacCready, who designed a human-powered "Gossamer Condor," generated ideas for his invention while reading about soaring birds. As he read, he realized that increasing the dimensions of a plane without increasing its weight would reduce the power needed to keep such a craft aloft.

Though many inventors are motivated by the thought of making money, more seem driven by natural curiosity and a desire to use their imaginations. They have the ability to visualize things they have never seen. In general, they are individualistic and optimistic, and seldom satisfied with the way things are. They tend to be confident, highly motivated free thinkers who persevere in their work. They believe there are no barriers they cannot surmount if they think hard enough and long enough. To bring an idea to fruition they will look at it and its consequences from all angles and sides.

Ideas often come to inventors and other creative people during moments of transition: while driving to work, relaxing, shaving, going to sleep, dreaming, or awakening. As a result, inventors learn to be alert to themselves in order to find the ideas from below the level of awareness that break fleetingly into the conscious mind. Such breakthroughs seem not to come during periods of intense concentration. Yet, hard work is essential to the sudden emergence of such ideas. Without an intense struggle with a problem in all its complexities, solutions never seem to surface.

How does an inventor prepare for his job? Many inventors will tell you that they exercised their curiosity when they were young. They learned to use their hands. They built telephones, made toy electric cars, constructed gadgets for the house, took motors apart, played with Erector sets, participated in science fairs, and did a variety of things using their hands and their heads simultaneously. In their formal schooling many had technical training, but it was often broad rather than narrow in scope. They took a variety of science, math, and engineering courses before concentrating on any one area of specialization.

THE STAGES OF INVENTING • Many inventors agree with the German scientist and inventor Hermann Helmholtz (1821–1894) that there are three stages in the inventing process. These stages are:

1. immersion,
2. incubation,
3. illumination.

In the first stage the problem is recognized (some would make this a separate stage) and investigated thoroughly. After a lot of toil, thought, and effort, some strange processes that are not well understood go on in the brain. Somehow, during this period of incubation, connections are made between ideas, facts, experimental data, and other knowledge stored in the brain. With time, luck, and attention to the glimmers that sometimes enter the conscious mind, an inventor reaches the stage of illumination. A new idea "pops out" and a solution to the problem is perceived.

When a solution becomes evident, it often seems so obvious that the inventor wonders why the incubation period took so long. It is then possible, in retrospect, to go back and suggest a logical set of steps leading from problem to solution. This is regarded by some as the final stage—verification. But the earlier stages—immersion, incubation, and illumination—seldom follow a logical, or vertical, line of thought.

WORKING AS AN INVENTOR • Once you have an idea for an invention, the first thing you should do is test the idea experimentally. Be sure it works! Next, make a small model of the device. As you build your model, ask yourself these questions: Who will be using the invention? How will they use it? Is it safe? How can I make it as easy to operate as possible? How can it be made most efficiently? What materials can be used to make it at the least cost and still be sure that it fulfills its purpose? Can it be manufactured for a reasonable price considering markups, the materials needed, and shipping costs? Is it marketable? Is it legal?

Next you'll need to build a prototype—a handmade version of the device that matches the manufactured form as you envision it. Should you want to sell your invention, a prototype will be valuable as a way of presenting your invention to a prospective buyer. Or, if you choose to manufacture the device yourself, a prototype will be helpful to engineers who plan the production process. Finally, you'll have to name your invention. Brainstorming may be useful here. You'll want a name that is catchy, descriptive, or both. It should be a name that's easy to say and remember.

Like Ben du Pont and other inventors, you should keep a detailed notebook of your ideas, data, experimental designs, sketches, and other pertinent information. Buy a spiral notebook with plenty of pages. If possible, buy one in which some of the pages are ruled for graphing. The graph paper will make it easier to make scale drawings, draw graphs, and record data in an orderly manner. The pages in the notebook should be numbered consecutively and notes should be in ink.

Not all inventions are machines. These large sand-filled barrels are a safety measure on many highways. If a car goes out of control or slides on ice and hits the barrels, the sand will absorb the car's energy more slowly than the concrete barriers.

Never erase information from the notebook. If you make a mistake, simply draw a line through the word or words and go on. Also, you should keep all sales slips and letters related to your work on the invention.

Periodically, have a witness sign and date the notebook. The witnessing should be notarized by a notary public. The reason for this is that the priority of an invention (should someone else file a similar application) can be sustained only by the testimony of someone else who will confirm that your statements are true.

NOW INVENT! • Look ahead to chapters 5 and 6. There you will find some problems designed to get you started as an inventor. Choose a couple that interest you and begin to think about them. Let the problems *incubate* for awhile as you read about inventions in history in chapters 2, 3, and 4. Don't forget to keep a small pad and a pen beside your bed. Like many inventors, you may think of possible solutions as you awaken, go to sleep, or dream. Don't kid yourself into believing you'll remember them the next day. The time to jot down those ideas is when you think of them.

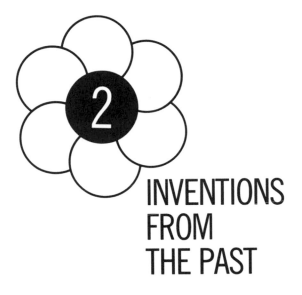

INVENTIONS
FROM
THE PAST

Humans have always been inventors. Many of the inventions that our ancestors made were ingenious and extremely useful at the time they lived. Today many of those inventions are seen only in museums. Our high-tech society has no use for them. For example, most people today have never seen a harness that was used to attach a horse to a plow or a wagon. Tractors are used to draw plows today, and the automobile long ago replaced the horse-drawn carriage.

INVENTIONS THAT ADVANCED CIVILI-ZATION • One of the characteristics of humans is their use of tools. Archaeolo-

23

gists have found that even the earliest humans were tool users. They made spears from wood; axes of flint and bone; fishhooks of flint, bone, and shells; and bows, slings, and boomerangs fashioned from a variety of materials.

About 4000 B.C. the plow was invented. The impact of this invention on human civilization was tremendous. With a plow to stir up the soil and irrigation from the rivers to keep the soil moist, one family could grow more than enough food for its own use. Since not everyone had to spend all of his or her time gathering or growing food anymore, specialization began. Some people became carpenters, potters, weavers, and scribes. They left the growing of food to others and sold or traded their skills or the products of their skills to farmers and other craftspeople.

At first, plows were pulled by humans. But by 3000 B.C., oxen were used to pull larger plows. When a way was found to make metals and then to mix them to produce alloys, someone realized that a plow made of bronze would last a lot longer and cut the soil better than a wooden plow. This allowed a single family to plant an even larger area, and, as a result, still more people could become specialists.

Certainly the wheel, which seems to have been invented about 3000 B.C., was another major breakthrough in human history. When the plow (now with wings to turn the soil) and the wheel were combined, the force needed to pull these larger plows required teams of oxen. Farmers began to share their animals and fields. Because people shared animals and tools, it made sense to live near one another. As a result, villages became more common.

Farmers then began to use horses to pull the plows because they were twice as fast as oxen. However, for horses to pull plows, someone had to invent the harness and collar. To walk on hard soil, horses' hooves had to be protected. So someone invented the horseshoe. To make horseshoes and attach them to the hooves of horses, a new job was created—that of blacksmith or farrier.

INVENTIONS OF WAR • In 1066 the forces of William the Conqueror won the Battle of Hastings in England. William's soldiers rode on horses equipped with a new invention—the stirrup. The stirrup allowed riders to stand up on their horses and effectively use spears while mounted. At the battle of Crécy in 1346, the English were decidedly outnumbered by the French. However, the English archers, who were armed with newly invented longbows, were able to shoot the mounted French attackers from their horses at distances as great as 400 yards. Consequently, the French were soon in retreat.

To combat the longbow, knights appeared in shining armor. But then Swiss pikesmen in tight formation carrying 18-foot-long ash poles tipped with steel spikes made knights on horseback obsolete. Then firearms ended the supremacy of pikesmen.

The invention of more and more terrible tools of war continued, culminating in the explosion of the atomic bomb over Japan in 1945. The atomic bomb and the hydrogen bomb that was developed during the cold war following World War II have the potential to destroy civilization. Perhaps more than anything else, fear of these weapons has prevented a nuclear war.

Though inventions have clearly influenced the history of human civilization, we have seldom been able to anticipate the effects they would have. For example, during the twelfth century the chimney was invented. It provided better heating, but it also led to changes in architecture. To reduce the amount of space heated, ceilings were lowered and rooms became smaller. Smaller but more numerous rooms led to more personal privacy. Bathing became more common and more frequent, and cleanliness and good manners came to be regarded as virtues.

Better heating allowed businessmen, scholars, and administrators to work year-round. Their increased activity stimulated the economy and led to more construction. However, increased construction led to a shortage of wood, which was needed both for construction and as a fuel for fireplaces. People began to mine and burn coal. Coal-burning furnaces and stoves were invented. These devices provided more efficient heating than fireplaces.

The temperature of burning coal made it possible to produce molten iron. The melted iron could be cast into various shapes. As a result, engine makers began replacing brass with iron as they built cylinders for steam engines. The growing importance of steam engines in the eighteenth century, coupled with a scientific interest in gases and their behavior, eventually enabled scientists and engineers to better understand the behavior and operation of engines and the fuels they burned. With the discovery of oil and the invention of the gasoline engine, a new and faster means of transportation became available. Trains and automobiles brought towns, states, and nations together. The airplane brought continents together. A century ago it would have taken all day, or longer, to travel from most homes to a major city. Today, you can journey halfway around the world in the same time.

SOME OLD TOOLS OF THE PAST • Earlier in this country's history, many of the tools shown in the photographs below were widely used. What was each one used for? See how many of them you can identify.

If you have trouble identifying these devices that were invented by your ancestors, perhaps your grandparents or great-grandparents will be able to help you. They might enjoy the challenge, and may be able to tell you stories about when and how many of these tools were used. (Answers can be found in the appendix on page 115.)

Four photographs (A–D) below show objects that were used in or near the kitchen.

Photograph E below contains three items. The largest one at the top of the picture was used in or near the kitchen. The other two tools were used by craftsmen. The tool at the bottom, between the handles of the other tool, would normally have a long handle, much like an ax handle, attached to it. The head of the handle, like the head of an ax handle, would fit into the opening that ends at the bottom of the tool as seen in the picture.

The next four photographs (F–I) are of tools different craftsmen used. Can you name the tool and the craft?

The next five photographs (J–N) show tools that were used on the farm. You might find one or two of these tools still in use on small family farms today.

The last two photographs (O, P) show tools that might have been found in various places around a farm a century ago.

Can you identify
these antique kitchen
implements?
See Appendix 3
for answers.

A

B

D

What were these used for?

E

F

G

H

I

Some of
these farm
implements
are still
used.

M

N

Your grandparents may have used these tools on the farm a century ago (see Appendix 3 for answers).

O

P

NOT ALL INVENTIONS ARE USEFUL • Patents are supposed to be granted for inventions that are useful, functional, and unique. The list that follows is a number of patent applications that were submitted to the U.S. Patent and Trademark Office. You will probably agree that these inventions are unique, but how many were useful and functional?

○ A grapefruit shield that prevents you from getting squirted with grapefruit juice when you put a spoon into the fruit. (But what about the others around the table?)

○ A solar powered fan built into a hat to cool the wearer's head. (Let's hope the fan was quiet.)

○ A parachute cap that fastened to your head with chin straps. This was combined with thick padded shoes that you wore on your feet. If you were caught in a burning building, you could jump out a window, pull the rip cord which opened the "head parachute," and hope that the thick soles would soften the impact when you hit the ground. (A user could enter tall buildings assured that he was prepared for the worst. It also helped if the user had strong neck muscles.)

○ A locket in which to store used chewing gum. (It was better than the bedpost!)

○ Safety goggles for chickens so they couldn't peck each other's eyes. (But how did the chickens clean their goggles?)

○ A hunter's blind in the shape of a cow to fool the birds. (Why not in the shape of a tree? The birds might have come to the blind to build a nest.)

○ A life-size wooden "horse" to attach to the front of a car (1900 model) so the car wouldn't frighten the horses which were still the main means of transportation. (But would a horse have expected another horse to say "cha-pa, cha-pa, cha-pa"?)

○ A child's swing that was to be used to supply the power for a washing machine. (Why waste all that youthful energy?)

○ A coffin complete with oxygen, food, and telephone. (Just in case the doctor was wrong.)

○ An automatic hat tipper. (For men with sore arms. Earlier in this century, when everyone wore a hat, it was common for a man to tip his hat when he met a woman he knew on the street.)

○ A convertible bedroom/piano that combined a piano, bed, sofa, and bureau. (For the pianist who slept a lot.)

○ A combination stepladder and ironing board. (Especially useful for the painter who ran a laundry.)

○ A dimple maker. (For those who thought dimples added to their appearance.)

THE STYLES
OF SOME
GREAT INVENTORS

Inventors such as Thomas Edison, Eli Whitney, Samuel Morse, and Alexander Graham Bell are generally regarded as rugged individualists who single-handedly arrived at their inventions. Many people consider these nineteenth-century individual inventors superior to today's corporate inventors who generally work in groups.

But in fact, no inventor has ever worked entirely alone. James Rumsey, John Fitch, and Robert Fulton all worked on steamboats. All of them benefited from the successes and mistakes of others who preceded them or worked at the same time. And none of them could have built a steamboat had not Thomas Savery, Thomas Newcomen, Oliver Evans, James Watt, and others designed and built steam engines.

Samuel Morse is generally given credit for inventing the telegraph. But it was Joseph Henry who showed Morse how to make an electric current move an electromagnet. Henry also invented the relay, which made it possible to send an electrical signal over long distances. Both men depended on the discoveries of scientists such as Volta, Ampère, Oersted, and Faraday, whose experimental research led to an understanding of electricity and magnetism.

Inventors have much in common, but they often approach problems in different ways and with different philosophies. There is probably something unique in every inventor's style.

LEONARDO DA VINCI • For centuries the world has regarded Leonardo Da Vinci (1452–1519) as one of the world's greatest painters. The faces we see in his *Mona Lisa* and *Last Supper* are amazingly real. Leonardo's notebooks, discovered in this century in old libraries, reveal that Leonardo was more than a great painter. He was an inventor, architect, botanist, ecologist, astronomer, mathematician, and anatomist.

Unfortunately for the world, Leonardo kept his ideas to himself. His notebooks are written in print that can be read only with a mirror. Did he fear the wrath of other scholars who held different opinions? Or was he keeping his findings secret until that day when he would at last understand the grand design of nature?

We now doubt he wrote in mirror image form in order to keep his ideas secret. Rather, because he was left-handed he probably found it easier to write from right to left.

His inventions, which were drawn in great detail in his notebooks, were often centuries ahead of their time. For example, he invented a four-wheel horseless wagon powered by two giant springs that were to be alternately wound by a "conductor" using a lever. Recognizing that wheels would have to turn at different speeds on curves, he circumvented the need for a differential by supplying power to only one wheel. His car was the forerunner of today's toy wind-up cars. Why don't we find spring-powered cars on today's highways?

He invented a wooden tank for warfare. The tank, made of heavy planks, had a cannon on each side, in front, and in back. It was mounted on four wheels powered by cranks turned by men inside. He invented a diving suit that would allow a diver to breathe air stored in a wineskin as he made his way to the bottom of the hull of an enemy ship. Once there, he could cut holes in the ship causing it to sink.

Some of his other inventions include a movable cam, a ratchet jack, a device for measuring the strength of wires, a machine for rolling copper and tin into sheets, a monkey wrench, a pair of pliers, a reciprocating saw, a pipe borer, a device for automatically feeding paper into printing presses, a needle grinder to mass-produce needles, a pedometer, a machine for stamping coins, a device for measuring wind speed, a worm gear, a pump to force water from deep wells or mines, a floating dredge to clear swamps, and a type of prefabri-

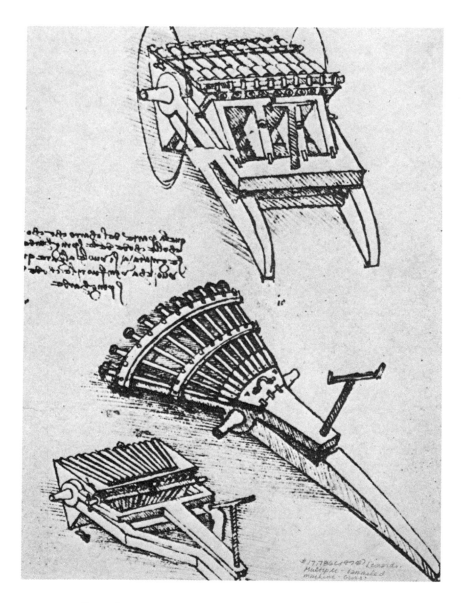

**Drawings for a multiple-barreled machine gun
from one of Leonardo's notebooks. While one set
of barrels fired, another could be reloaded.**

cated housing. He developed cord drives. In his note-book he wrote, "Every motion machine with cords is quieter than one that is made with toothed wheels and pinions." He thus anticipated today's belt-driven machines. Da Vinci was surely an inventor ahead of his time!

He was a man of opposites. He despised war and spoke of it as "bestial madness," but served Cesare Borgia as an engineer during Borgia's military campaigns in 1502. Though he bought caged birds in order to set them free and refused to eat flesh because he opposed the killing of animals, he designed automatic spits powered by falling weights to roast meat. He painted the *Mona Lisa* and the *Last Supper,* but also sketched the gory details of war and hangings. He seemed to be fascinated by the extremes inherent in human nature.

LEONARDO'S STYLE OF INVENTING ◦ For Leonardo, nature held all the great designs. His intense curiosity led him to conduct careful observations and investigations as he attempted to understand nature's grand plan. To design airplanes, he studied birds in flight. To design submarines, he watched fish as they swam. He sought to design machines that functioned as efficiently and automatically as the living bodies found in nature. Leonardo saw a machine as a living body—a series of parts, all working together. He recognized that though a machine might consist of gears, pulleys, belts, chains, screws, levers, connecting rods, cams, ratchets, and other parts, as a whole it was more than the sum of its parts. Like so many inventors, Leonardo was able to find similarities or likenesses among things and ideas that for most people were totally unrelated.

To better understand the working and structure of the human body, he dissected cadavers, drawing detailed sketches of what he saw, including the heart and its internal structure. His notes reveal that he wondered how the heart might be made to work better, for Leonardo was a perfectionist. He was never satisfied with his inventions or his paintings. He would come back to them and see ways to improve them. His notebooks contained dozens of ways to convert reciprocating (back-and-forth) motion to rotary motion and vice versa—work that preceded similar efforts by James Watt to build a steam engine by 300 years.

With time Leonardo would always see ways to improve everything he invented. So, in a sense, he never finished anything. His perfectionism prevented him from feeling that he had ever really succeeded. His curiosity about everything constantly distracted him from one investigation to another. He lacked Thomas Edison's perseverance because his interests were far broader. He had no great desire to make money. He sought to understand the grand scheme of the universe, not the solution to a single pressing problem.

Above all, Leonardo's style was visual. He had a superb ability to observe and to see every detail in the things he viewed. This is evident in his paintings where we see every line, every eyelash, every detail in the subject's expression. His uncanny eye for detail enabled him to see each and every flaw in his paintings. A century before Galileo showed that a projectile follows a parabolic (curved) path, Leonardo's sharp eye enabled him to see and sketch the paths of cannon balls. He knew they did not rise and then suddenly fall, as many believed.

His keen vision was coupled with a vast imagination and an outstanding ability to visualize. In his mind he could "see" the solution to problems and then transfer his mental images onto paper. Beside his drawings he would write detailed operating directions. His ability to coordinate hand, eye, and mind to visualize a better solution to a problem for which he had devised an invention has probably never been equaled.

His style can also be characterized as scientific. His artistic eye for detail led him to the realization that details are important in understanding nature as well. We cannot understand nature or solve problems solely by reasoning from general principles. His studies led him to understand that many of the established principles about nature, as stated by the scholars of his day, were false. He recognized that generalizations about nature could be made only by finding common threads among a large number of specific examples (called "inductive reasoning"). Given enough specific observations, we may find a common principle that explains all the individual details.

Leonardo's scientific approach to nature led him to conduct a number of experiments that were well ahead of his time. For example, he designed experiments to measure frictional forces 300 years before Coulomb conducted similar studies. He discovered that frictional forces depend on the nature of the surfaces in contact and the weight of the moving object but are independent of the area of contact. He also found that friction

duced by increasing smoothness or by using
or lubricants.

's work—as scientist, inventor, and artist—
___ ue genius is revealed by his understanding
that knowledge comes from our ability to draw conclu-
sions from what we see and extend them to what we
cannot see.

THOMAS ALVA EDISON • Thomas Edison (1847–1931)
was a poor boy who achieved fame and fortune through
hard work. He had only three months of formal
schooling before his mother, dissatisfied with his
teacher, decided to tutor him. Under her guidance he
became a voracious and rapid reader who could remember almost everything he read.

Before he was ten, Edison had a lab at home. When
he was twelve years old, he took a job as a newsboy and
candy seller on a 7:00 A.M. train from Port Huron to
Detroit. During the midday hours, as he waited for the
train to make its return trip, Edison devoured science
books in a Detroit public library. He set up a small
laboratory in one of the train's baggage cars. The igni-
tion of some phosphorus that started a fire on the train
forced him to dismantle his until-then secret laboratory
and nearly cost him his job.

When he rescued a small boy who had strayed onto
the railroad tracks, his life took an unexpected turn. The
boy's father, who had no money but wanted to reward
Edison, offered to teach him telegraphy. Edison learned
quickly and soon became the fastest telegraph operator
in the country. In 1868 his work in telegraphy brought
him to Boston. While there he found a workshop where
he could work on his ideas for inventions.

He soon obtained a patent for a device that recorded votes automatically. Edison made a journey to Washington to present his idea to a Congressional committee. The committee, however, decided it did not want to see the workings of Congress streamlined. They rejected the idea of using Edison's invention to increase the speed of legislative voting. Their decision led Edison to vow never again to invent an unwanted gadget.

The following year he sought work in New York City. While waiting for an interview at a stock brokerage office, their telegraph machine broke down. Edison quickly repaired it and was offered a job as an assistant to the firm's electrical engineer. His work on Wall Street gave him enough money to live as he worked on his next invention—a stock ticker that could send stock prices across the country. He sold the patent rights for the ticker to a large stock firm for forty thousand dollars, about eight times as much as he had expected to receive. With the money he set up a plant in Newark, New Jersey, to manufacture the machines and their tapes.

In 1876 Edison built a laboratory in Menlo Park, New Jersey. He hired a number of assistants to work in what was essentially the country's first industrial research laboratory. Long hours and hard work led to an invention that improved the telephone, allowing it to be used for long distance communication. Also from Menlo Park, in rapid succession, came the phonograph, the dictating machine, and a telegraph system that allowed four messages to travel along a single wire. Edison soon became known as the "Wizard of Menlo Park." His growing fame enabled him to attract the funds he needed to embark on the project for which he is best known—a practical incandescent electric light bulb.

As he began his research, Edison realized that if these bulbs were to illuminate millions of homes, three things were needed: a very good vacuum within the bulbs; a bright, long-lasting filament; and a means of generating large amounts of electrical power. Therefore, he divided his staff into three groups. One group, headed by Ludwig Boehm, worked on techniques for creating a better vacuum within the bulbs. Another group tackled the problem of building a dynamo that could supply high voltage at a constant level. A third group investigated filaments that might be used in the bulbs. Their search involved testing 1,600 kinds of filaments including metal wires, cloth, paper, hair, threads, fishline, cork, and punk.

By the summer of 1879 Boehm had been able to obtain vacuums as good as one-millionth of an atmosphere. Edison then turned to carbon filaments because he knew that carbon had the highest melting point of any element. On October 21, 1879 they tried cotton thread packed with carbon. In his notebook Edison wrote, "No. 9 ordinary thread Coats Co. cord No. 29, came up to one-half candle and was put on 18 cells battery permanently at 1:30 A.M. . . . No. 9 on from 1:30 A.M. until 3:00 P.M.—13½ hours and was then raised to 3 gas jets for one hour then cracked glass and busted."

His success led Edison to say, "If it can burn for that number of hours, I know I can make it burn a hundred." He later found that a certain kind of cardboard packed with carbon would glow for approximately 170 hours.

Like all inventors, Edison depended on other people, though he tended to take all the credit for the inventions developed at Menlo Park. Francis R. Upton, an electrical engineer at Menlo Park, realized that a low-resistance, low-voltage, high-current system could not be used on any large-scale lighting project. The cost of the required copper wire would make electrical power too expensive for all but the very wealthy. As a result, Edison instructed the team working on dynamos to build 100-volt generators. By increasing the voltage ten times, the current could be reduced to one-tenth and the resistance raised a hundredfold by using wires one-tenth as thick. Such a system reduced the cost of copper to one hundredth of what it would have been with a 10-volt system.

The men who had invested in Edison's electric light project became impatient as Edison continued his "cut-and-try" (experimental) method. They felt he was creating a toy that would never have any practical value. In December 1879, Grosvenor Lowry, a patent lawyer who was a fan of Edison, leaked a story about Edison's work to *New York Herald* writer Marshall Fox. Fox published a major piece praising Edison and predicting that electricity would soon replace gas as the major source of lighting in cities. The public, excited by Fox's article, clamored to see the product. In order to appease his financial backers, Edison announced that he would open Menlo Park to the public on New Year's Eve. He quickly set up a dynamo and a few dozen lights so that more than 300 enthusiastic sightseers could see the new year (1880) and a new and brighter future open under the electric lights at Menlo Park. Edison's electrical system, together with more than a thousand of his other inventions, changed the face of the world within half a century.

Edison was neither the first to develop electric lights or dynamos to generate electricity, nor to invent an incandescent light bulb. But he was the first to develop a practical and economic means of bringing electric lighting into domestic use.

EDISON'S STYLE OF INVENTING ○ Early in his career Edison established six rules that he felt were essential to the process of inventing.

1. Define the need for an innovation. Never invent something that isn't needed. (He learned this lesson from his voting machine.)

2. Set a goal and stick to it.

3. Analyze the stages needed to reach your goal and follow them.

4. Make all the data on the progress toward the goal available to all who are working on the same invention.

5. Give each member of the inventing team a well-defined area of activity.

6. Record all data and ideas related to the invention so that all such information can be examined at a later date.

Edison's mania for invention is evident from his remark, "I can never pick up a thing without wishing to improve it." Leonardo would have agreed, but he was such a perfectionist that he was never fully satisfied with anything he had done and frequently revised his inventions.

An early advertisement for Edison's phonograph

Edison was more practical. He knew his invention could be improved, but it was a lot better than anything else he'd seen. And it would sell!

Unlike Leonardo Da Vinci, Thomas Edison *did* want to make money. He claimed to have no use for curiosity unless it had the promise of financial gain. In fact, he had great disdain for intellectuals and abstract ideas. When someone suggested that he was a scientist, Edison replied, "A scientist busies himself with theory. He is absolutely impractical. An inventor is practical." He went on to say, "Anything that won't sell, I don't want to invent. Its sale is proof of utility, and utility is success."

Edison lacked Leonardo's visual and artistic ability, but he frequently made drawings of the machines he proposed. For Leonardo, the idea, or a careful drawing of the idea he visualized, was sufficient, but Edison preferred to work in a more concrete setting. He liked to build models of his inventions so that he could get his hands on the results of an idea and manipulate it. Edison's cut-and-try method involved taking real things, such as possible bulb filaments, and trying them one by one to find the best solution.

Edison claimed to be uneducated, but actually he was self-educated and read extensively as he worked on projects. His favorite book, Michael Faraday's *Experimental Researches in Electricity,* was always close at hand.

Because he lacked a formal, technical education, he often did not know that the invention he was working on was considered impossible by the "experts." He was so stubborn he would never consider failure. When someone referred to him as a godlike genius, he replied,

"Godlike nothing! Sticking to it is the genius." His well-known quote, "Genius is one percent inspiration and 99 percent perspiration," may best reflect his attitude toward the inventing process.

Though he tended to think in concrete terms, Edison's thinking, like that of many inventors, was unconventional. He regarded hard thinking as the vital ingredient of inventing. It was exhausting but essential. His laboratories were filled with constant reminders to his workers. A quote from Joshua Reynolds was one of his favorites, "There is no expedient to which a man will not resort to avoid the real labor of thinking."

R. BUCKMINSTER FULLER • Buckminster Fuller (1895–1983) was as much a philosopher as an inventor. He believed that man was part of a universal plan, put here to discover "principles governing the eternal interrelationships existing between various extraordinary phenomena." The laws of science, such as the law of gravitation, as viewed by Fuller, "manifest the eternal intellectual integrity of the Universe that I speak of as 'God.' "

Because no other organism has the capacity to discover the laws that reveal the design of the universe, Fuller believed that humans exist "for some cosmically important reason"—a reason that we must think about in a cooperative and global manner. Because humans have a mind, argued Fuller, they can invent tools that allow them to extend themselves and do things that other life forms cannot. Through their minds, the human species can come to understand the grand plan of the universe.

Fuller referred to this ability to eventually understand the "whole" of the universe as *synergy*. To Fuller, synergy meant the behavior of the whole system, a behavior which could not be predicted by knowledge of the component parts or any subassembly of components. For example, one cannot predict the properties of water (hydrogen oxide) from its components, hydrogen and oxygen. Hydrogen is a flammable gas and oxygen supports combustion. Yet water, a compound of hydrogen and oxygen, is used to extinguish fires.

Fuller thought of Earth as a spaceship with a swimming pool cruising through space at an enormous speed while rapidly turning. In our spaceship we transfer an enormous amount of energy, 95 percent of which is wasted. Yet, all that energy is but a ten-billionth of the total energy Earth receives from the universe. The fossil fuels were, he believed, simply a means of starting the "main engine." Because we are depleting our supply of fossil fuels, we must learn to use them at a rate equal to or less than the rate at which they are forming. This means that we must use natural energy sources such as the sun, wind, water, gravity, and tides. To eliminate our dependence on fossil fuels, we must use our minds to invent the tools and methods that allow us to use free, natural forms of energy wisely and efficiently.

Fuller believed that we are at a critical time in our history. If we do not learn to use natural sources of energy, we are doomed. However, he firmly believed that the human mind will find solutions that enable us to eliminate the need for fossil fuels. Eventually, we will learn to use the energy that comes to us in abundance from the rest of the universe (primarily the sun). Then we will be able to devote more time and effort to our ultimate purpose—finding the grand plan that governs the universe.

FULLER'S INVENTING STYLE ○ Though Fuller was not motivated by money, he did share Edison's optimism. He believed that inventions and technology will save humanity, not destroy it. In the process of inventing, he felt, we will learn how to work the "levers" of our magnificent universe.

Fuller is best known for his geodesic dome, which required only a thousandth as much weight as earlier domes of equal size. He also invented the first stream-lined car, the dymaxion house—a light, prefabricated structure that could be transported by air, prefabricated bathrooms that were hung on light frames, and a variety of building designs that you can find in the book, *Inventions: The Patented Works of R. Buckminster Fuller.*

Fuller believed that inventors should use their minds to enhance all humankind, rather than to make material gains at the expense of others. Unlike Edison, he believed that the discoveries of pure science were the raw materials of inventors. Rather than spurning scientists, he sought their help. Fuller, however, did share Edison's cut-and-try method. He believed that inventors were bound to make many mistakes, but that they could learn from them. Mistakes, he believed, often led to insights that would not have come in any other way.

Fuller's guiding principles were purpose and economy, not beauty. He wrote, "I never try to anticipate what my structures are going to look like. I am concerned only with providing comprehensive, logical, pleasingly adequate, and the most economical solutions to all design problems. . . . Beauty to me must be a product result and not a purpose."

IRVING LANGMUIR • Irving Langmuir (1881–1957) was a research scientist who won the Nobel Prize in chemistry in 1932. For many years he worked for General Electric. Some of his discoveries enabled that company to manufacture better electric light bulbs. His research revealed that tungsten filaments in bulbs partially filled with nitrogen were brighter and lasted longer than any other kind.

By finding a means of producing superior vacuums (pressures less than a billionth that of the atmosphere), Langmuir enabled GE to mass produce the "hard" vacuum tubes used in radios. His studies in monolayers (films a single molecule in thickness) led to thorium-oxide-coated tungsten cathodes that provided thousands of times more electrons per second than earlier vacuum tubes.

Despite his obvious value to General Electric, Langmuir, unlike Edison, never did research with a practical goal in mind. Like Leonardo, he was motivated by curiosity alone. GE recognized that the best thing to do with Langmuir was leave him alone, and it paid off!

From the work of Fuller, Langmuir, and Edison we see that the process of inventing can follow from diverse styles, attitudes, and philosophies. Whether driven by a concern for the destiny of man as a part of the universe, curiosity, or profit, very different inventors can all generate inventions that have a profound and lasting effect on society.

There do seem to be certain traits that are common to all inventors. They all use cut-and-try methods, at least part of the time. They think hard, and in unconventional ways, finding common factors in seemingly unrelated things and ideas. All agree that keeping detailed records of what they do is useful. Visualizing and drawing what they visualize seems to be a valuable ability, though some can do it better than others. Also, despite the fact that profit is a motivator for some, they are all curious about things around them and seem driven by a desire to bring about improvements. They all learn from their mistakes, regarding errors as a natural part of the process of inventing.

Most likely, as you begin to invent, you'll arrive at a style of your own. It may include the best traits of these inventors that you have read about, but it will probably be unique—in ways that you may not even be aware of until you reflect upon it. You may even benefit from something that can't be gauged or predicted—luck!

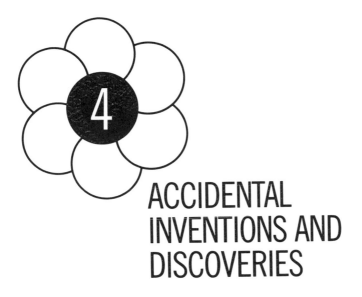

ACCIDENTAL
INVENTIONS AND
DISCOVERIES

Many people think scientific research and inventing are processes in which logic and careful thought lead to earth-shattering discoveries and inventions. It's probably because, when writing about the work that led to a discovery or invention, scientists and inventors present the story as a series of logical steps.

There is no question that logic, discipline, persistance, and brilliant thinking are vital to scientific inquiry and inventing. Nevertheless, inventing and scientific inquiry are seldom linear processes. There are gaps, frustrations, blind ends, backtracking, and, infre-

This invention found in the marshes of
Cape Cod may have been discovered by
accident. Biting flies enter the box at
the bottom and become trapped inside.

quently, sudden unforeseen success—the "Aha" that drives inventors and scientists to continue their work. It is the occasional thrill of discovery that enables them to endure the many failures which are far more frequent than the few successes we hear about.

If you read the detailed accounts or notebooks of a variety of scientists and inventors, you will be struck by the number of discoveries and inventions that are made by accident. Of course, it takes a well-prepared and open mind to recognize the importance of the accidental result, effect, observation, or mistake.

NEW FOODS BY ACCIDENT • Potato chips, for example, appear to have been invented by accident in the summer of 1853 by George Crumb, a chef who worked at Moon's Lake House in Saratoga Springs, New York. A guest who was dining in the restaurant complained that the french fries were too large. The waitress brought the potatoes back to George who cut them in half and fried them once more. The guest was still not pleased, so George cut them in half again. Still the diner complained, whereupon George, hoping to rile the diner, took his sharpest knife and cut the potatoes into strips as thin as he could make them. He then fried them until they were so crisp one could not even stick a fork into them. To the chef's dismay, the result so pleased the guest that he praised George's work to other dinner guests. Soon, Saratoga Chips, as George came to call them, became an attraction at Moon's Lake House and in other localities.

Others found that after the french fries had cooled, they were still tasty. As a result, cold Saratoga Chips became popular in some areas. However, it was not until the invention of the mechanical slicer in the 1920s that potatoes could be thinly sliced in quantities large enough to make potato chips a national treat.

Here's the story of another accidental discovery. Richard Blychenden was attempting to promote the sale of a blend of Indian tea at the St. Louis Exposition in the summer of 1904. It was so hot, however, that no one wanted to drink tea. A bored Blychenden happened to pour a cup of his brewed tea over some ice chips. He found it to be a refreshing, cool drink. Once he began serving his customers this new drink, his business boomed. Thousands of thirsty fair-goers clustered about his booth drinking Blychenden's invention—iced tea!

Earlier, another tea salesman, Thomas Sullivan, was searching for a different way to send samples of his tea to prospective customers. The tins he had been using to ship the tea were expensive, so he decided to send the samples in small silk bags. The customers, however, thought the small bags were a new way of brewing tea. Presto! Sullivan had accidentally and unknowingly invented the tea bag.

In the late nineteenth century, Dr. John Harvey Kellogg and his brother Will directed the Battle Creek Sanitarium in Michigan, a health spa that advocated a vegetarian diet. In an effort to make this diet less bland, the Kellogg brothers organized a food laboratory. Here, among other things, they searched for substitutes for the flavors of beef, pork, and chicken that they could incorporate with the grains and vegetables that constituted the bulk of their diet.

During one of their experiments, they were trying to invent a low-starch, whole-grain bread by boiling wheat. Responding to an emergency call, they left the laboratory for two days. They returned to find a pot of soggy boiled wheat that had cooked far too long. They decided to process the wheat-mush anyway by running it through flattening rollers. The Kelloggs were surprised to see the result. Instead of a sticky flat sheet, each wheat berry had turned into a small flake. When these flakes were toasted, they provided a delicious, cold breakfast cereal.

The Kelloggs then experimented with rice and corn as well as more wheat. By accident they had discovered wheat flakes, rice flakes, and their now famous corn flakes. They received a patent for their process of "tempering" grain in 1894.

There are thousands more examples to demonstrate that discovery is often a matter of accident. There are also probably thousands more accidents that could have led to important discoveries or inventions had the inventor or scientist taken the trouble to observe or consider the accident with greater care.

AN ACCIDENTAL MEDICINE • Before you begin to think that accident plays a role only in such trivial cases as the discovery of good things to eat, let's look at the story of penicillin. In 1928 Alexander Fleming was growing a pus-forming bacteria, a species called *Staphylococcus aureus*. Because of poor technique, Fleming found a mold on one of his bacterial cultures. Unlike many bacteriologists who might simply have discarded the culture, Fleming noticed that the bacteria around the mold were dead. Following up on this accidental discovery, Fleming began growing cultures of the mold. He was able to identify the mold as *Penicillium notatum*. Fleming found that the mold, *P. notatum,* killed a number of other bacteria in addition to *S. aureus.* But there were other species of bacteria that were not affected by the mold. Fleming also tested the mold with mice, rabbits, and human blood cells. None were harmed by *P. notatum.*

During World War II there was a great need for antiseptics to treat soldiers wounded in warfare. Dr. Howard Walter Florey read Fleming's research reports and decided to try to extract the key ingredient in the mold that was able to kill harmful bacteria. He succeeded in extracting what he called penicillin from a vat of the mold and its nutrients. He later found that the calcium and sodium salts of penicillin were more stable than the extract itself. Further, he found that these salts could cure certain infections in mice. After tests on human subjects proved successful, the antibiotic was produced on a large scale at the Northern Regional Research Laboratory in Peoria, Illinois. It saved countless lives during and after the war. Penicillin was the first of a number of antibiotics that have served medicine well.

SCIENCE AND ACCIDENTS • The history of science is filled with stories of accidental discoveries. One occurred in 1819. While preparing a demonstration for a class, Hans Christian Oersted placed a magnetic compass near a wire connected to a battery that was carrying an electric current. To his surprise, the compass needle moved. He was surprised because up until that time scientists had found no connection between electricity and magnetism. By experimenting, he found that the compass needle pointed in a direction perpendicular to the direction of the current. He moved a compass, which indicates the direction of the magnetic force, around a wire carrying an electric current. He found that the magnetic force was directed in circles about the wire. By accident, Oersted had discovered that a magnetic field encircles an electric current.

Later, in 1831, physicist Michael Faraday was searching for the opposite effect—a way to produce an electric current from a magnetic field. He had placed large magnets near wires, had wound the wire into coils, and had done a number of other things with no success. Then he happened to move a wire near a magnet. Suddenly, his meter indicated a current in the wire. But the current was present only when the wire or the magnet moved. Careful experimentation led Faraday to realize that a current was produced in a coil of wire only when the magnetic field through the coil was changing.

In 1927, C. J. Davisson and L. H. Germer were studying the reflection of electrons from a nickel target in a vacuum tube. The tube was broken by accident and the hot nickel reacted with the oxygen in the air and was immediately covered with an oxide coating. In an effort to remove the oxide, the nickel was heated at a high temperature for a long time. When the experiment was resumed, Davisson and Germer found that the reflecting properties of the nickel had changed. The new piece of nickel, they found, consisted of several large crystals of nickel instead of many small ones. They decided to see what would happen if they reflected electrons from a single crystal of nickel. To their surprise, the electrons were reflected in a manner similar to what we see when light is diffracted. When light passes through a series of very narrow openings placed side by side, the light spreads out into a series of bright and dark bands. This property of light is referred to as diffraction. It can be explained only by assuming that light behaves like waves. Davisson and Germer's results showed that matter, in this case electrons, can be diffracted and therefore have wave properties. For discovering this effect, which had been predicted by Louis de Broglie a few years earlier, Davisson received the Nobel Prize in physics in 1937.

Henri Moissan failed in his search for a way to make artificial diamonds by heating carbon. But while trying other materials in combination with carbon, he accidentally produced calcium carbide, from which acetylene gas can be made. A similar, but less important accidental discovery occurred when researchers at Dow Corning produced Silly Putty while seeking a way to produce artificial rubber during World War II.

In 1839, Charles Goodyear was looking for a way to treat rubber so that its texture would not change drastically with changes in temperature. In cold weather the rubber became brittle and stiff; in summer's heat, the rubber became soft and sticky. Goodyear, who had mixed sulfur and white lead with gum rubber, accidentally spilled some on a hot stove. When the glob on the stove cooled, Goodyear found that the substance remained rubbery over a wide range of temperatures. He had accidentally discovered a means of processing rubber that became known as vulcanization.

5

INVENTING
NEW USES
FOR COMMON
OBJECTS

Now you've had a chance to review the inventing styles of several of the world's greatest inventors. You learned about the traits that characterize most inventors, the tools they use, the way they think, and the role that accidents play in their work. It's time to begin working and thinking as an inventor yourself. You can begin by inventing some new uses for common objects.

Have you ever used a table knife as a screwdriver? Plenty of people have. On many desks you'll see a clothespin used to clip notes together, not to hang up clothes. At a party you may have noticed toothpicks used to pick up meatballs, pieces of cheese, and other kinds of food. Old inventions often acquire new uses, uses for which the invention was not originally intended.

NEW USES FOR COMMON OBJECTS • Listed below are a few objects that are common to almost all households. See if you can invent ten new uses for one or more of them. Begin by choosing just one. Hold it; feel it; study it; twist it; turn it around, upside down, and inside out. Look at it from every conceivable angle. As you do these things keep in mind that you're looking for new uses. Don't be upset if you can't generate ideas immediately. Inventing takes time. You may have to let your observations incubate for awhile. Most inventors do. Invent ten uses for:

- clothespins—other than for hanging clothes on a clothesline
- hairpins—other than for holding hair in place
- safety pins—other than for holding clothes together
- straight pins—other than for hemming clothes
- toothpicks—other than for picking or cleaning teeth
- paper plates—other than for holding food
- paper bags—other than for holding groceries
- marbles—other than for playing marble games
- insulated coffee cups—other than for holding hot drinks
- soda straws—other than for drinking liquids
- coat hangers—other than for supporting and hanging clothes

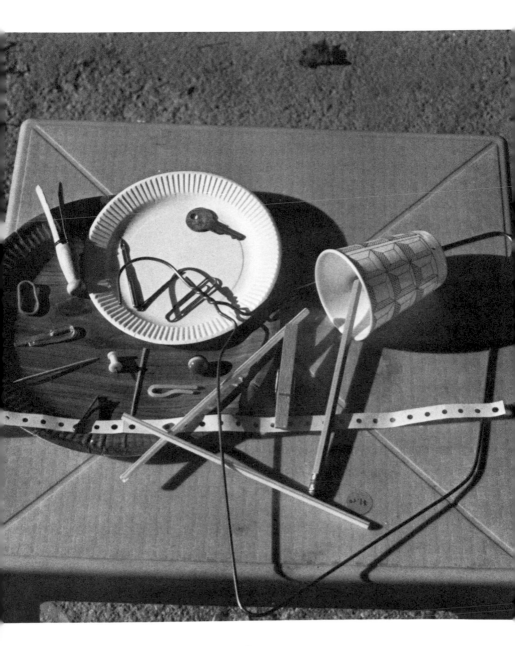

See if you can invent new uses
for these common items.

- paper clips—other than for holding papers together
- pencils—other than for writing
- tennis balls—other than for playing tennis
- pill vials—other than for holding pills
- pieces of Velcro—other than for holding clothing together

How did you approach the problem? Do you have a method or style of your own? Or did you borrow a style from one of the inventors you have read about?

What other common objects can you use to perform tasks they were not originally designed to do?

NEW USES FOR USED THINGS • We often discard empty cardboard milk and egg cartons. But some people put empty egg cartons on a workbench, and use them to hold different types of screws, tacks, pins, washers, nails, and other small items. Others cut up milk cartons and use them to make toys, grow seeds and plants, do experiments, feed birds, or any number of other functions. Inventing uses for old items will not only stimulate your creativity, it will enable you to reduce the amount of trash you throw away. In fact, once you've finished this exercise you might like to begin to think of ways to

Can you invent new uses for old articles such as these instead of throwing them away?

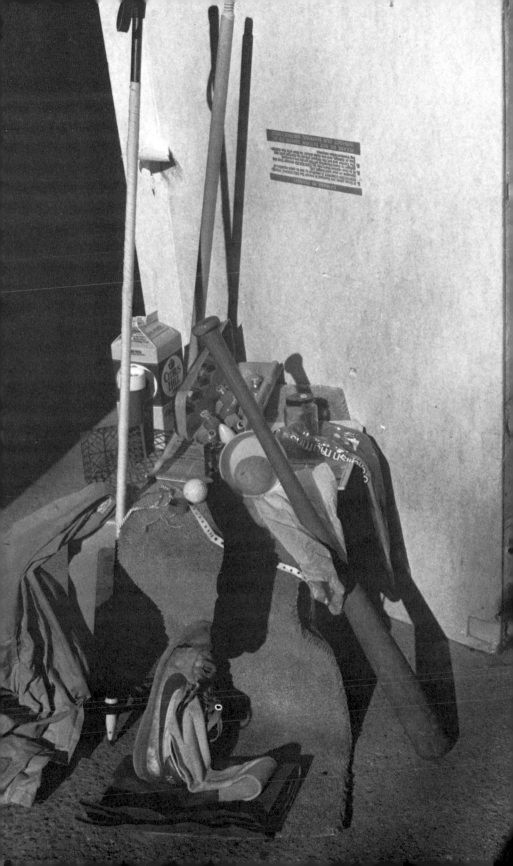

solve the nation's trash problem, which has arisen from the "throwaway mentality" that permeates our society.

As you approach the task of finding ways to use old objects, consider how Da Vinci, Edison, and especially Fuller might have dealt with this challenge. Then decide whether to use one of their approaches, a combination of approaches used by these great inventors, or your own method.

What uses can you find for these items?

- Broken broom handles
- Old or outgrown shoes, boots, or sneakers
- Old or worn-out clothes
- The perforated sides of continuous computer paper
- Worn-out automobile tires
- Cardboard boxes
- Empty milk cartons
- Empty egg cartons
- Broken baseball bats
- Empty baby food jars
- Rubber bands
- Old flashlights
- Dead flashlight batteries
- Worn-out tennis balls
- Cut golf balls
- Empty frozen juice cans
- Empty berry boxes
- Small pieces of soap
- Empty film containers
- Extra pieces of carpet

- Paper grocery bags
- Plastic bread bags
- The tie bands used to seal plastic bags
- Old newspapers
- Plastic food containers

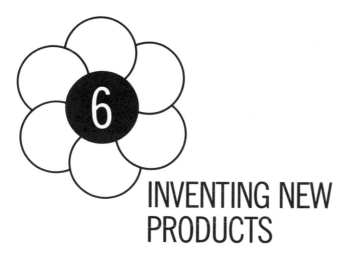

INVENTING NEW
PRODUCTS

As you have seen, inventions are sometimes stumbled upon by accident. However, we often hear people say, "I wish someone would invent a _____." In such a case, necessity may well be the mother of invention.

In this chapter you'll be challenged to invent things for a specific need or purpose. You won't be able to invent devices for all the challenges presented, but perhaps you'll succeed with some of them. Before you begin any one of them, think about how Edison, Da Vinci, or Fuller would have gone about solving the problem. Perhaps their styles will give you some useful clues. On the other hand, your mind may have its own unique mode of thinking that will lead you along a different creative path.

Whatever approach you use, be sensible with regard to *safety*. Do not take chances. **Seek the help of a knowledgeable adult when you need to use electricity, flames, or any articles or techniques that could be dangerous.**

In the list of "needed" inventions that follow the ones that would be regarded as less challenging are presented first. The more challenging (and perhaps impossible) inventions are farther down the list. Of course, something that appears impossible to one inventor may seem simple to another. Your task and challenge is to choose any of these needed products and invent it. Good luck!

See if you can invent a (an):

○ device for squeezing tea bags
○ better duster for dusting a house
○ device for cleaning and/or dusting venetian blinds
○ recipe for a casserole
○ better book bag
○ "face muff" to go with ear muffs
○ "nose muff" to go with ear muffs
○ indoor hose that attaches to a faucet for watering indoor plants
○ automatic device for watering indoor plants
○ device for threading thread through a needle
○ doormat that really takes all the mud and dirt off shoes, even shoes with grooved soles
○ device for cleaning chalkboard erasers

- device for picking pickles from a jar
- opener for tight jar lids
- mechanical trash picker-upper
- socks with hard toes so it won't hurt when you stub your toes
- waterproof pockets
- press-on removable pockets
- pickpocket-proof pocket
- pickpocket alarm
- clothes that expand as children grow, or shrink as adults lose weight
- way to use all the lipstick in a lipstick tube
- game the entire family can play
- modified miner's hat for people who like to read in bed
- book holder for reading in bed
- page turner for disabled readers
- automatic bed maker
- better egg carton
- best color combination (letters and background) for visibility on a sign
- pen that allows you to mix inks within so that the same pen can be used to write in different colors
- homemade toy car powered solely by a mouse-trap
- better "waker-upper" than an alarm clock
- system that allows young children to dial a bed-time story
- longer lasting light bulb (**Be sure to have a knowledgeable adult work with you on this one. Household circuits can be very dangerous.**)

- fog-proof mirrors for bathrooms and steam rooms
- stable food tray for eating in cars
- way of cooking food in the can it comes in
- carbonator that attaches to the kitchen faucet so that you can obtain carbonated water with ease
- messages that can be read only with a mirror
- art form that serves a useful purpose, such as a painting that tells time or a piece of sculpture that serves as a lamp
- new inexpensive but effective way to insulate buildings
- thermostat control that automatically changes thermostat settings at different times of the day so as to use less energy in heating your home **(Work with a knowledgeable adult on this one.)**
- way to identify what's inside chocolate candies
- sunburn alarm that beachgoers can attach to their bathing suits
- device for removing pins that fall onto a rug
- spoon holder that prevents spoons from slipping into a dish or bowl
- comfortable but supportive office or study chair
- device for squeezing toothpaste evenly from the bottom of the tube
- device that will automatically raise and lower the flag on a flagpole
- way to reduce the cost of making hot water in your home
- side piece for lawn mowers so trimming and mowing can be done at the same time
- soft sink in which dishes will not break
- pedal-powered snowmobile

- automatic means of separating glass, metal, paper, plastic, and other material commonly found in trash
- artificial ice that will allow people to skate in the summer without the expensive refrigeration techniques used to make ice
- natural means of air-conditioning a home or apartment
- livelier baseball
- pitching machine that simulates a real pitcher
- skis that will slide on grass, sand, and/or pavement for those who want to ski year-round
- robot to paint steeples, flagpoles, and skyscrapers
- robot that will referee or umpire sporting events
- way to prevent poison ivy
- spray-on or paint-on sterile surgical gloves that would quickly solidify and that could be peeled off easily
- way to open car doors when the keys are locked inside
- paper-processing machine that will change waste paper into useful forms such as writing, tracing, wrapping, and tissue paper
- bacteria that will act on plastic and convert it to biodegradable matter. (**Seek the help of a professional biologist for this project. Some bacteria can cause disease.**)
- "uncopy machine" that will remove print and drawings placed on paper by a copy machine so that the paper may be reused
- dream machine—a VCR for sleeping brains

- tiny camera computer keyboard that allows you to print date, time, location, and subject on each frame when a photo is taken
- electronic road map that will keep a car on course
- artificial gills that will allow people to breathe underwater
- compact, portable machine that converts water vapor in the air to potable water
- room where weightlessness prevails for training astronauts
- flush toilet that will work in a spaceship
- flush toilet that will work underwater
- spaceship kitchen and dining room
- way to produce oxygen on long space trips to Mars and other distant planets
- way to use the materials found on Martian and lunar surfaces to produce oxygen and other materials needed in a space colony

ANOTHER INVENTOR'S STYLE ● One inventor whose style we have not discussed is Rube Goldberg. Perhaps you have seen drawings of a Rube Goldberg invention. You have probably heard someone say, "That's a real Rube Goldberg device."

Rube Goldberg (1883–1970) was educated as an engineer, but he left engineering to become a cartoonist early in his adult life. Many of his cartoons satirized America's preoccupation with technology; his name became another way of indicating that some simple process had been made complicated beyond belief. In his cartoons, it was Professor Lucifer Gorgonzola Butts who devised the outlandish inventions. Butts's automatic stamp licker consisted of a small robot who tipped over a bottle of ants onto a sheet of postage stamps that lay upside down on a table. Near the stamps was an anteater who had been starved for three days.

Just for fun, you might enjoy inventing some Rube Goldberg devices of your own. Or you may prefer to just draw them. Here are some Rube Goldberg devices you might try to invent. Make them as outrageously complicated as possible.

- A burglar alarm
- A fan
- A light switch
- A doorbell
- An automatic door opener

AN
INVENTION
CLUB

According to Harvard University's Project Zero, a study of cognitive skills in the sciences and humanities, there are certain traits that are shared by creative people:

- A desire to find or create beauty. For an artist, beauty may be created by painting a sunset; for an inventor, by developing a logical and original solution to a problem.
- Interest in unusual questions or in asking unique questions of their own. Creative people thrive on novelty and uncertainty. They really enjoy the strug-

gle to find solutions to the challenging puzzles they confront or create.

○ A capacity for metaphor. They are able to make connections among seemingly unrelated things, events, or ideas in order to solve difficult problems.

○ A willingness, perhaps a need, to challenge traditional assumptions.

○ Objectivity. Though excited by their work, creative people step back and test, judge, and evaluate periodically as they proceed. As one scientist has said, "It's easy to think up a great many ideas. The tough part is eliminating the bad ones."

○ Willingness to take risks. In fact, creative people enjoy living "on the edge" of their competence. Certainly, this was true of Thomas Edison. We can marvel at what he accomplished, especially in view of his limited background in science and engineering. Yet, no one enjoyed the challenge of a problem more than Edison. Nor was he hesitant about taking risks, whether with money or ideas.

○ Motivation from within. Inventors and creative people tend to be driven by curiosity. To most of them, money, grades, awards, and recognition are not important.

Because these traits do not appear to be genetic, it may be possible to teach creativity. Many people think it is possible; others do not. The activities of an invention club may not answer this difficult question. However, such an organization may either teach people to be creative or remove the barriers that prevent them from realizing their natural creative bent.

STARTING AN INVENTION CLUB • If your school does not have an invention club, you and a few of your friends who are interested in inventing might like to organize one. Talk to your principal, assistant principal, science teacher, shop teacher, or someone else at your school who might be interested in helping you with such a club. If no one in your school can help you, you might be able to find a parent, an engineer, a patent attorney, or maybe even an inventor in your community who will work with your club.

A number of schools do have invention clubs. A few have courses in inventing or creativity. Therefore, it makes sense to call a number of other schools in your area or state. See if they have such a program or know of schools that do. When you locate such a school, you might arrange to visit with the person in charge. Find out how they went about organizing their program. If possible, attend one or two of their meetings. Talk to them about their activities. What do they do? How do they attract members? How often do they meet? Have they held an invention fair? Who sponsors it? Do they know of inventors who might be willing to talk to your club?

THINGS TO DO AT AN INVENTION CLUB MEETING • As you have read, certain traits seem to be characteristic of inventors. One of the purposes of an invention club is to try to develop these traits and to practice the kinds of thinking and working that are essential to inventing. The club gives you an opportunity to think unconventionally in the company of others who recognize its value.

One activity that members may enjoy is finding new uses for common objects (see chapter 4). Stanley

Mason, inventor of the disposable diaper and the squeezable ketchup bottle, is reported to have once said, "A safety pin is simply a straight pin bent in a different way." Thinking about how to use common objects in new ways may lead to some useful inventions. Even if it doesn't, it will at least help you begin to think like an inventor.

Steven Caney's Invention Book and *The Unconventional Invention Book* by Bob Stanish are good sources of ideas for things to do (see "For Further Reading"). It might be a good idea at an early meeting for members to agree to locate as many useful books as possible. At a later meeting, the task of reading these books and culling out activities and ideas that would be valuable to the club could be divided up among the members.

Those activities useful to an invention club could be assigned to different members. At subsequent meetings each member could lead a workshop that made use of one or more of the activities that club members agree are worthwhile.

Another activity that is very useful for inventors who work in small groups is brainstorming. You might even want to brainstorm about the topics that might make good subjects for brainstorming. One way to begin such a session is to have the group make a list of all the ways in which a coat hanger or a milk carton might be used. In the brainstorming process accept *all* ideas, even the wildest ones. The ideas can be written on a chalkboard, an easel, or large sheets of paper taped to the wall. Try to get everyone to participate, and don't quit. Keep working. Stick to it.

The value of brainstorming can be seen in an incident reported by Fritz Henning in his book, *Concept and Composition*. A group was trying to find a way to hide tanks and other military vehicles from high-flying enemy planes that were taking photographs of the terrain below. The method had to be fast, within ten seconds after the plane was spotted.

During the brainstorming, one man suggested copying the way a quail responds upon seeing a hawk. He leaped to the floor and stretched out his arms mimicking the quail. "Why does the bird spread its wings?" asked a participant. "To diffuse (spread) the shadow of his shape," said another. Immediately, the group realized that shadows cast by vehicles would show up on photographs taken from the air.

Someone suggested a tarpaulin. But others objected, "Too slow!" "Balloons!" was another idea. It was followed by, "Party favors that are blown. They unreel." This idea eventually led to a solution. A series of light-weight plastic tubes were to be coiled in a package atop each vehicle. They could be filled with gas from a compressed air tank within seconds, producing a spaghettilike camouflage that covered the vehicles.

Once you've brainstormed to find new uses for a common object such as a coat hanger or a milk carton for half an hour or more, you may want to see if some of the ideas can be combined. Can new ideas emerge by combining old ones? Sometimes just changing the order or arrangement of the idea list will give rise to a new thought. Or you might focus on one use that most members agree is a good one. Use that idea to practice some other kinds of thinking that inventors use. Consider what the new device might be used for if it were turned around, turned upside down, inside out, right for left, positive for negative, etc.

The group might also look at ways to improve one of the ideas. What can make it better? Why does it need to be improved? Of the several or more ways to improve it, which one is best? Why? Can it be made still better?

Practicing such things in brainstorming sessions will help members develop the kind of creative thinking needed for inventing. It will help you to realize that you do have original ideas. All of us do. The problem is that we tend to say, "Oh, someone must have thought of that already."

Many people mistakenly believe their ideas are not important. As a result, they keep their ideas to themselves. Don't do that! Let others know about your ideas. You'll find you can contribute unique ideas. Once you see that others listen to you, you'll express your thoughts with greater confidence, regardless of how "far out" they may seem. And as your confidence grows, your ideas are likely to become more unique and creative.

By brainstorming with other club members, you will come to realize that lots of ideas can be generated if you focus on something. You'll learn to see how flexible thinking—looking at all the possibilities of an idea by viewing it from all sides and angles—can lead to modifications that make a good idea even better. You'll see that generating unique and novel ideas may also arise from the interaction of a variety of thoughts and plans. By discovering how concentrating on the details of one idea or device can lead to its improvement, you will acquire the confidence you need to tackle the process of inventing on your own. Finally, having fellow members to whom you can turn for advice and help is yet another valuable function of an invention club.

OTHER ACTIVITIES FOR AN INVENTION CLUB •

There are a number of other, more specific activities that members of an invention club might do. Some of them may seem "off the wall" to you at first. But remember, inventors tend to be unconventional thinkers. It's not likely that you can become an inventor by thinking only in a logical fashion. Lateral thinking seems to be an essential trait for all inventors. The following are a few activities that your club may want to try. You can find more in the references mentioned above.

Relaxing. Since creative ideas often come during periods of transition—going to sleep, awakening, dreaming, relaxing—it might make sense to begin a club meeting with relaxation exercises. While lying on your back, contract the muscles of your hands and feet. Then let these muscles relax. Next, contract your legs, then your arms. Let these muscles relax, in turn. After repeating this process a few times, contract all the muscles of your body for a few seconds. Then, let the muscles relax. Repeat the process several times. Finally, relax and let your mind go. You may find that creative ideas more frequently arise when you are in this relaxed state.

Analogies. Fill in the blanks in the sentence: "How is _____ like _____?" For example, how is a candle like a light bulb? Or you might use simple word analogies such as, day: night : : light: ?. Which is read, "Day is to night as light is to _____." Members fill in the blank.

Let each member propose one or more analogies. Then choose one at a time and see how members modify one another's analogies. After a number of people have modified an analogy, you might also ask, for example, "How is a candle *unlike* a light bulb?"

Here's another form of analogies: which is better, a Δ or a □? Or which do you prefer: = or ≠?

Obviously, members can use creative thinking not only to solve such analogies but to create them as well.

Synthesizing. Think of things that might be improved by adding to it or modifying it in a particular way. For example, what could be made to look better by rounding its edges? Or, what would be better if it were painted red? Made smoother? Cut in half? Turned around?

Imagining. Try to imagine what it would be like to be something you never could be. For example, describe what it would be like to be an oxygen atom, or an electron in a copper wire.

Imagine you are walking, wading, or swimming through deep mud, Jell-O, a swamp, pudding, sand, shallow water, fly paper, etc. Move the way you would if you were in one of these substances.

Puzzling objects. Try to visualize the answer to each puzzle by "seeing" the solution in your mind. Then actually try it with real materials.

Can you make a quarter pass through a hole the size of a penny? (Try it using a sheet of paper.)

How many identical spheres can you arrange in such a way that *they all touch each other?* How many identical coins can you arrange in such a way that they all touch each other? How many cylinders can you arrange in such a way that they all touch each other? (Answers, in same order, 4, 5, 6, [or 7 if one cylinder is perpendicular]) Is there a shape that will allow 8 to touch one another?

Imagine a cube made of 27 smaller wooden cubes, each 1 centimeter on a side. Thus, the dimensions of the cube will be 3 cm × 3 cm × 3 cm. Now, the outside surfaces of the cube are to be painted red. How many cubes will remain unpainted? How many will have just one of their six surfaces painted? How many will have two surfaces painted? Three surfaces painted? Will any be painted on more than three sides?

A mirror image. Place a mirror upright on the page above these two words:

CHOICE

QUALITY

Why does one word, seen in the mirror, appear to be upside down and not the other?

Word puzzles. Here are some word puzzles that you may find fun and thought provoking. Can you figure out what they mean?

(a) $\dfrac{\text{EZ}}{\text{iiiiiiiiii}}$ (b) $\dfrac{\text{Black}}{\text{Coat}}$

(c) $\dfrac{\text{Man}}{\text{Board}}$ (d) $\dfrac{\text{Knee}}{\text{Light}}$

(e) $\dfrac{\text{Wear}}{\text{Long}}$ (f) $\dfrac{\text{Stand}}{\text{I}}$

(g) $\dfrac{\text{iii} \quad \text{iii}}{\text{O} \quad \text{O}}$ (h) Le
vel

(i) $\dfrac{\text{O}}{\begin{array}{c}\text{L.L.D}\\\text{M.D.}\\\text{Ph.D.}\end{array}}$ (j) Dice   Dice

(k) ecnalg   (l) /R/e/a/d/i/n/g/

(m) cycle cycle   (n)   R
Road
o
d

(o) Me   Quit   (p) He's I Himself

(q) T   (r) T   (s) Hurry ↑
o   o
u   w
c   n
h

(For answers, see page 117 in appendix 3.)

Cartoon captions. Collect some cartoons and make copies so each member can have one of each. Cut off the cartoonist's captions and ask members to write their own. Then compare the results.

Ink blobs. Place a blob of India ink on a piece of paper. Use a straw to blow the ink in different directions. When the ink has dried, what do you see in your "drawing"? What do others see? What do you see in their work?

Painting with words. Cut out colored words and letters from magazines. Use them to "paint" a picture.

Sharpening your senses. Sit in a quiet room. Listen carefully. Make a list of all the sounds you hear. Which ones can you identify? Which remain unknown? Afterward, compare your results with several other club members who are doing the same thing.

Again, sitting in a quiet room, make a list of all the odors you can smell. Which ones can you identify? Compare your results with others who are doing the same thing.

Look at a burning candle for ten minutes. Make a list of all the things you observe about the candle. Compare your results with others who are observing the same or a similar candle.

Mirror movements. Stand face-to-face with a partner. Pretend that you are your partner's mirror image. Respond appropriately to all your partner's motions. Then let your partner be your mirror image.

AN
INVENTION
FAIR

Once your club is organized and there is enthusiasm for inventing among the members, you may want to consider organizing an invention fair. By then, members will be familiar with the kind of lateral, unconventional thinking that inventing requires. They'll know how to let their minds roam as they think about a problem. They'll know how to brainstorm, how to generate many solutions as they set about solving a problem, and how to pick the best solution by cut-and-try methods.

ORGANIZING A FAIR • You can't hold a fair unless there's a place for it. You or the adult who supervises your invention club will have to talk to your principal or superintendent. It's quite possible that your school will let you use the gymnasium or hallways at no cost if you explain the benefits of such an event. If you're required to pay for custodial care and/or supervision, you may be able to find a custodian who will volunteer his or her time. Perhaps a teacher or principal will supervise the event. In any case, you will probably have to find a way to raise money. Perhaps a local business or businesses will help defray costs. Or you may have to organize bake sales, sell raffle tickets (if legal), or find some other way to raise funds.

Unless you have a large number of members, you will probably want to open the fair to all students who are interested in exhibiting their inventions. Decisions will have to be made regarding the extent of the fair. Will it include all grades? Will schools from other towns or districts be invited to participate? Posters and announcements will have to made well in advance of the scheduled date of the fair to allow participants sufficient time to prepare. Also, it will be necessary to prepare, print, and distribute application forms to those who wish to enter the competition. Then someone must see to it that all the applications are reviewed.

The nice thing about an invention fair is that it need not involve all the formal reports and preparation normally required by participants in a science fair. Most of the work, once an idea for an invention has been generated, is the hands-on business of building and testing the device. Of course, each participant should prepare a brief report explaining his or her invention, as well as a poster to attract people to the booth or table. If the

Scenes from an invention fair

invention is too large to bring to the exhibit hall, then a working model should be prepared for the fair.

Well in advance of the fair, your club will have to find people to serve as judges. You will probably be able to find people in the community who are willing to volunteer as judges if you give them plenty of advance notice. Teachers, patent attorneys, engineers, businessmen, college and university professors, artists, computer programmers or engineers, writers, and people from a variety of other professions might be asked to serve in this capacity. Preferably they should be people who have some experience with inventions or creative thinking.

If prizes are to be awarded, you will have to raise the funds to pay for them. If the competition is open to students of all ages, prizes for different age or grade levels should be awarded.

Shortly before the scheduled date, club members must know how many tables or booths to set up to accommodate those participating. You'll need to send reminders to the judges, alert local newspapers, step up publicity, and, if possible, arrange to use an auditorium for the presentation of prizes.

INVENTION FAIR INVENTIONS • If you've been a member of an invention club for some time, you probably have plenty of ideas for inventions that you could enter in a fair. If you're a recent member or you don't belong to a club, it may take some time for you to come up with an idea. Reading this and other books related to inventions and inventing will help, but it's still not an easy task to design a winning invention.

Often, young inventors get their ideas from their own needs. One girl noticed that her mother complained of backaches after mopping the kitchen floor. To help her mother she invented a foot mop. It consisted of large sponges wrapped in cloths that fit over her mom's shoes. Her mother could then mop the floor by simply sliding her feet.

In 1873, at the age of fifteen, Chester Greenwood of Farmington, Maine, had great difficulty keeping his ears warm while skating in Maine's severe winter cold. His hat kept blowing away or falling off and his ears, which had been frostbitten, were very sensitive to the cold. In response to this personal need, Chester took a long piece of heavy wire and twisted its ends into two large loops. He asked his grandmother to sew pieces of heavy cloth over each loop. Greenwood had invented earmuffs.

By 1877 he had obtained a patent for his invention. He went on to build a factory that manufactured his patented earmuffs. Greenwood's success with his first invention so excited and interested him that he became a full-time inventor. During his life, he was granted a hundred more patents. But he is best known for ear-muffs, an invention that he made to satisfy a personal need. Among the inventions on display at a recent inven-tion fair were wrist mittens (see photo, p. 98). Perhaps they also arose from a personal need. How about peel-away paper plates designed to cover sturdier plates?

Perhaps the one-handed kitchen helper came from another inventor whose parent had a sore back. (Combi-nation tools have been an inventors' paradise since the invention of tools.) Coffee bags are a fairly common

**Exhibits
at an
invention
fair**

invention-fair invention, but how are they better than instant coffee? Reusing greeting cards as postcards seems like a unique idea, and braille money for the blind is a good idea. Do you think they are patentable?

OTHER INVENTION CLUB EVENTS • In between your club's annual invention fairs you might like to hold a few less formal, but equally challenging contests that require the use of the same skills that go into inventing. A tower contest and a bridge-building contest are two that you may find will generate interest and enthusiasm among contestants. However, your club can probably invent a number of original contests of your own design once you become active inventors.

A TOWER CONTEST ○ Get together with others in your school or neighborhood to organize a tower contest. Give a prize to the person who can build the tallest tower from a fixed number of toothpicks, soda straws, clay, clothespins, paper clips, or some other common "building block," such as Popsicle sticks. You might also allow contestants to use some predetermined combination of such items.

You will have to establish a set of rules for the contest. For example, will glue, pins, or some other means be used to connect the basic building blocks? Should the contestants be limited to a fixed number of building blocks or to a fixed weight of such materials? A fixed-weight rule, for example, would allow them to use either flat or round toothpicks. You might allow contestants to choose their own construction materials but set a limit on the final weight of the tower. In that way they could use any combination of materials such as tooth-picks, clothespins, and glue or clay and soda straws, or paper clips, clothespins, clay, and soda straws, and so on.

A BRIDGE-BUILDING CONTEST ○ A similar contest might be organized to see who can build the strongest bridge. For example, a contestant might be allowed one box of toothpicks or a hundred Popsicle sticks and one tube of glue. With just these materials, the challenge is to build a bridge spanning a one foot gap that will support the largest load. Again, your club can decide on the rules, including what materials may be used and in what quantity.

By now you should be well on your way to inventing a variety of devices, modifying common items for other purposes, or finding new uses for old articles. If you want to be an inventor, you're off and running. However, whether you become an inventor or not, using your mind creatively, thinking in unconventional ways, brainstorming, and keeping careful records of what you do will be useful to you in any vocation you may choose.

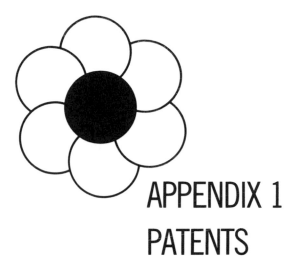

APPENDIX 1
PATENTS

The United States Constitution states in article 1, section 8, "Congress shall have power . . . To promote the progress of science and useful arts, by securing for limited times to authors and inventors the exclusive right to their respective writing and discoveries."

PATENTS: PROTECTION FOR INVENTORS • Congress passed an act creating a patent system in 1790. To be patented, an idea or invention must be a machine, a process, an article of manufacture, or a composition of matter. To be accepted by the Patent and Trademark Office (PTO) the invention must be new, useful, and functional.

On February 2, 1790 the first patent commission was established. It consisted of Henry Knox, the secretary of war, Edmund Randolph, the attorney general, and Thomas Jefferson, the secretary of state, who himself invented a pedometer, a swivel chair, and an improved plow. After a careful examination, the first patent was granted to Samuel Hopkins for a new apparatus and process for making certain chemical compounds.

After 1793 an examination of the patent was no longer required. One could receive a patent by submitting an application and paying the $30 fee. Without an examination, applicants were expected to have conducted their own investigation to see if a patent for their invention already existed. Few applicants bothered to conduct such a study. As a result, there were many conflicts regarding claims for patents. In 1836, John Ruggles of Maine rose in the Senate to state, "Many patents granted are worthless . . . and conflict upon one another. . . . People copy existing patents, make slight changes and are granted patents. Patents have become of little value, and the object of the patent laws is in great measure defeated."

Ruggles's speech led to the patent law of 1836. This law required a thorough examination of all applications to be certain that the invention was new, useful, and operational. The law also required that each application be accompanied by a working model of the invention. In less than forty years the patent office had filled all its available space with the many models that had been submitted. As a result, starting in 1870 models were no longer required unless requested.

The purpose of patents is to encourage the creativity of inventors, to help promote the development of inventions, and to give inventors (or companies) the opportunity to profit from their inventions. By receiving a patent an inventor agrees to make public the details of his or her invention so that anyone can build a working model of the invention. The patent office will then publish the patent so that other inventors and scientists will have that information available to them. Such knowledge might be useful to them in their own research and development. In fact, someone reading about a particular patent might contact the inventor and try to purchase the patent rights.

Through a patent, an inventor obtains the exclusive right to make and sell the innovation for a certain period of time. The time period depends on the invention. *Utility patents*, which include mechanical and electrical devices, are granted for a seventeen-year period. *Design patents* may be for three, five, seven, or fourteen years. These are novel and original designs or stylings of existing things, for example, a bicycle made to look like an airplane. *Plant patents* are also granted for seventeen years. These are new plants developed by crossbreeding.

On April 4, 1988, the first animal patent was granted. It was awarded to Harvard University for a "transgenic nonhuman eukaryotic animal" to be used in cancer research. By genetic engineering these animals, usually mice, can be made very susceptible to cancer-causing agents. As a result, much smaller quantities of these cancer-inducing substances will be needed in cancer research.

The holder of a patent has the right to keep other people from making or selling the patented invention for a certain period of time. It does not mean, however, that the PTO will police a patent. Selling, licensing, or preventing others from copying a patent is the inventor's responsibility. As a result, some people or companies prefer to keep their discoveries secret because they fear it will be impossible to police them, or they believe they can keep the secret from others for longer than seventeen years. The formulas for Coca-Cola and Silly Putty, for example, have been kept secret for many years.

A patent gives an inventor the opportunity to reap a monetary profit if the invention is translated into a commercial reality. However, the success of the patented invention depends on what the inventor does with it.

If an invention is made known to the public before it is patented, the inventor has one year in which to apply for a patent. After that, no one, including the inventor, can obtain a patent for the device.

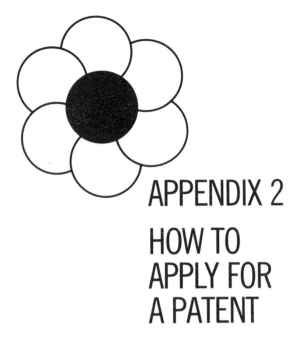

APPENDIX 2
HOW TO
APPLY FOR
A PATENT

Approximately 100,000 applications for patents are filed each year. About three-fourths of them are made by people who work for large corporations. Here are two publications that will help you apply for a patent:

Patents and Inventions: An Information Aid for Inventors. This guide can help you decide if you have an invention that could be patented. It also tells you how to apply for a patent. Write to:

Superintendent of Documents
U.S. Government Printing Office
Washington, D.C. 20402

The Official Gazette of the United States Patent and Trademark Office, a weekly publication that can be obtained from the same source, lists all the patents that have been granted in a particular week, patents that are available for sale, and any changes in the rules for obtaining a patent. You can obtain a year-long subscription or buy single issues of the gazette. The document is useful for checking to see if a patent for an invention similar to yours has been issued in recent months.

APPLYING FOR A PATENT • Applying for a patent is not a simple process. If you think you have an invention that could be patented (patents for perpetual motion machines will not be accepted), it would be wise to contact a patent agent or a patent attorney. (The names of such people in your area can be found in the yellow pages of a telephone directory for a major city.) For a fee, he or she can help you decide whether your invention is worth the cost involved in obtaining a patent.

If you file an application for a patent, you must prepare a document describing your invention. The document should explain how your invention is unique and useful. It should also include technical drawings to show you how it's made and how it works. Finally, you must sign an oath stating that you are the original inventor, and you must pay the necessary fees.

It takes several years for the patent office to do a thorough search to be sure your invention is original and to decide if it is useful and operational. Consequently, you, or a company that buys your patent rights, might choose to market your invention marked "patent pending." This should be done only if a patent attorney has conducted a thorough search and is certain that no similar patent has been issued. Once a patent is awarded, all copies of your invention should be marked "Patent No." followed by the number of your patent.

For a more detailed description of how to apply for a patent, see *Steven Caney's Invention Book* or *How to Patent and Market Your Own Invention* by Marvin Grosswirth.

A SAMPLE PATENT APPLICATION • An example of an application for a patent is shown below. It was filed by Michael Sylvester of Foam Seal, Inc. in Cleveland, Ohio. Large portions of the application have been left out to save space, but you can see how it meets the requirements mentioned above.

DOUBLE-HUNG SLIDE-BY WINDOW UNIT

ABSTRACT OF THE DISCLOSURE

A prefabricated window unit with a combination polyurethane foam/polyvinyl chloride foam strip between all or portions of the inner assembly and outer supporting frame characterized by greatly improved resistance to air and moisture intrusion.

BACKGROUND OF THE INVENTION

This invention relates to insulation strips and seals for between the inner and outer sill plates, the

---

inner and outer headers, and the side rails and the jambs of prefabricated window units.

. . . In the past, various types of sealing means have been used in windows. Fibrous material and open-cell flexible foam provide good thermal insulation but permit some air intrusion. Plastic weatherstripping prevents air intrusion, but does not provide good thermal insulation. . . . [o]nly flexible open-cell foam permits the desired amount of thermal insulation and compressibility. The open-cell foam, however, does not prevent the intrusion of air and moisture.

SUMMARY OF THE INVENTION

The object of the invention is to provide a flexible, resilient sealing strip for a prefabricated window unit which provides good thermal insulation qualities and good compressibility, and, at the same time, prevents air and moisture intrusion through the sealing strip.

In accordance with the invention, . . . the resulting sealing strip may be compressed as much as one-half of its thickness, due to the compressibility of the polyurethane open-cell foam portion, and yet intrusion of air and moisture is prevented by the outside closed-cell polyvinyl chloride foam portion.

BRIEF DESCRIPTION
OF THE DRAWINGS

FIG. 1 . . .

FIG. 2 is a fragmentary, sectional view, taken on the line 2–2 of FIG. 1;

FIG. 3 is a fragmentary, sectional view on an enlarged scale, taken on the line 3–3 of FIG. 1 . . .

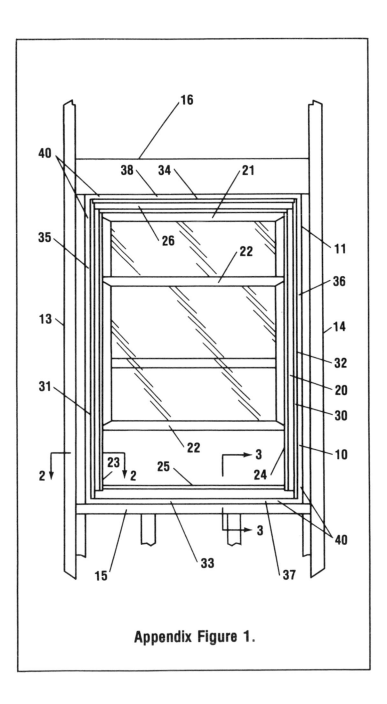

Appendix Figure 1.

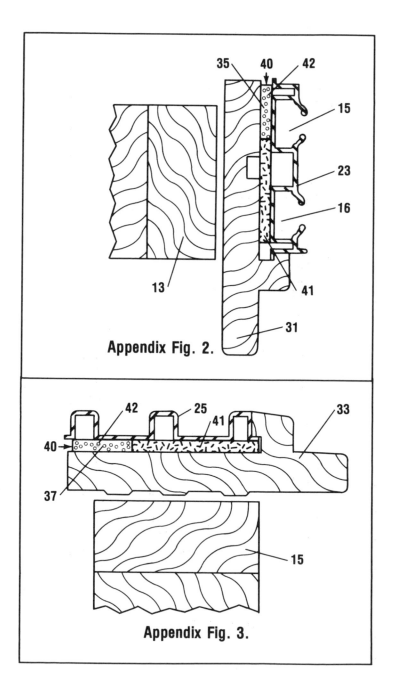

Appendix Fig. 2.

Appendix Fig. 3.

DESCRIPTION
OF THE PREFERRED
EMBODIMENT

Referring more particularly to the drawings, and initially to FIG. 1.

The rails 23 and 24, inner sill plate 25, and inner header 26 are formed of vinyl extrusions which may have any number of configurations, such as the typical configurations illustrated in FIGS. 2 and 3.

The composition and manufacture of polyurethane foam are well known in the art. A suitable polyvinyl chloride foam for use in the present invention may be made up as follows:

The surprising advantages of the present invention are illustrated by the following experiment:

A window made by the Semling-Menke Company, of Merrit, Wisconsin, was tested in a wind loss test facility in which a window unit was subjected to an air pressure differential. The commercial unit, with a polyurethane foam strip, had a pressure drop of 30%. A unit with a strip of the PVC foam and polyurethane foam adhered together had a pressure drop of less than 10%. A unit with a strip made up entirely of PVC foam had a pressure drop of less than 5%.

[A] combination polyurethane and polyvinyl chloride foam strip . . . retains the desirable compressibility characteristics of the open-cell polyurethane foam while adding the weather resistance and impermeability to air and moisture of the closed-cell polyvinyl chloride foam. . . .

The resulting product of the present invention provides optimum thermal insulation and optimum resistance to air and moisture intrusion through the insulating material, and also permits sufficient compression so as to provide all of the desired characteristics outlined above. . . .

While the invention has been shown and described with respect to a specific embodiment . . . the patent is not to be limited in scope and effect to the specific embodiment herein shown and described, nor in any other way that is inconsistent with the extent to which the progress in the art has been advanced by the invention.

WHAT IS CLAIMED IS:

1. In combination, a prefabricated unit adapted to be installed in an operative position opening defined by rough frame members of the outside wall structure . . . unit having an inner assembly and an outer supporting frame, and a flexible resilient sealing strip made of foamed plastic material adapted to be installed between at least some portions of said inner assembly and outer supporting frame, said strip comprising an outside portion of a flexible closed-cell polyvinyl chloride foam material.

2. A sealing strip for use around the inner assembly of a prefabricated unit . . . the open-cell portion having good compressibility characteristics.

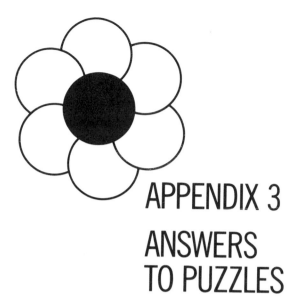

APPENDIX 3
ANSWERS
TO PUZZLES

ANSWERS TO PHOTO PUZZLES
ON PAGES 28–34

A. This device was used to boil eggs. Eggs were placed in the holes and the whole device was placed in a boiling pan. The small sand clock enabled the chef to measure the cooking time.

B. A coffee grinder.

C. This machine was used for making mayonnaise. The oil dripped into the bowl along the wire seen in the funnel.

D. This is a spigot. It fit into the bunghole of a barrel and was used like a faucet.

E. At the top is a washboard. It was used for scrubbing clothes.

The item with two handles is a draw blade that carpenters used for shaving and shaping wood.

At the bottom, lacking its handle, is an adze. It was used to smooth large timbers used for beams.

F. This tool, called a froe, was used to cut wooden blocks into shingles.

G. This is a pickaroon. It was used by loggers to turn logs.

H. It's a butteris. It was used by farriers to pare the hooves of horses before they were shoed.

I. These are ice tongs. They were used to carry blocks of ice.

J. Scythes like this one were used to mow tall grass.

K. This bit was placed in a horse's mouth. The chains were connected to reins (lines) held by the driver. The bit and reins enabled the driver to control and direct the horse.

L. Corn planters like this one were used by farmers in the late spring. The lower end of the planter was pushed into the soil. When the machine was tipped forward, the springlike device seen at the bottom left opened a chute that allowed corn seed to fall into the ground. The farmer walked along placing several seeds into the soil with each step.

M. Once the corn was grown, a corn knife like this one was used to cut the stalks, which were then tied into bundles.

N. This bale hook or box hook was used to lift or drag heavy items such as bales of hay.

O. This lantern probably burned kerosene or alcohol. Supposedly the great Chicago fire was started by a cow that kicked over a lantern.

P. This balance was used to weigh various things including meat, milk, and grain.

ANSWERS TO WORD PUZZLES ON PAGE 90

(a) Easy on the eyes.

(b) Black overcoat.

(c) Man overboard.

(d) Neon light.

(e) Long underwear.

(f) I understand.

(g) Circles under the eyes.

(h) Not on the level.

(i) Degrees below zero.

(j) Paradise.

(k) Backward glance.

(l) Reading between the lines.

(m) Bicycle.

(n) Crossroads.

(o) Quit following me.

(p) He's beside himself.

(q) Touchdown.

(r) Downtown.

(s) Hurry up!

FOR FURTHER READING

Brown, Kenneth A. *Inventors at Work*. Redmond, Wash.: Tempus Books, 1988.

Burke, James. *Connections*. Boston: Little, Brown & Company, 1978.

Caney, Steven. *Steven Caney's Invention Book*. New York: Workman Publishing, 1985.

Cooper, Margaret. *The Inventions of Leonardo Da Vinci*. New York: Macmillan, 1965.

Crump, Donald J. *Small Inventions that Make a Big Difference*. Washington, D.C.: National Geographic Society, 1984.

Fuller, R. Buckminster. *Inventions: The Patented Works of R. Buckminster Fuller.* New York: St. Martin's Press, 1983.

————. *Operating Manual for Spaceship Earth.* New York: Pocket Books, 1973.

Gies, Joseph, and Frances Gies. *The Ingenious Yankees.* New York: Crowell, 1976.

Grosswirth, Marvin. *How to Patent and Market Your Own Invention.* New York: David McKay Company, Inc., 1978.

Henning, Fritz. *Concept and Composition.* Cincinnati: Northlight Publishers, 1983.

Heydenreich, Ludwig H., Bern Dibner, and Ladislao Reti. *Leonardo the Inventor.* New York: McGraw-Hill, 1980.

Laithwaite, Eric. *Engineer Through the Looking Glass.* London: British Broadcasting Corporation, 1980.

Ray, William, and Marlys Ray. *The Art of Invention: Patent Models and Their Makers.* Princeton, N.J.: The Pyne Press, 1974.

Sobel, Robert, and David B. Sicilia. *The Entrepreneurs: An American Adventure.* Boston: Houghton Mifflin Company, 1986.

Stanish, Bob. *The Unconventional Invention Book.* Carthage, Ill.: Good Apple, Inc., 1981.

Stanish, Bob, and Carol Singletary. *Inventioneering.* Carthage, Ill.: Good Apple, Inc., 1987.

Stein, Ralph. *The Great Inventions.* Ridge Press/Playboy Press, 1976.

Sutton, Caroline. *How Did They Do That? Wonders of the Far and Recent Past Explained.* New York: William Morrow and Company, Inc., 1984.

Weiss, Harvey. *How to Be an Inventor.* New York: Harper & Row, 1980.

Williams, Trevor I. *The History of Invention: From Stone Axes to Silicon Chips.* New York: Facts on File, 1987.

Wilson, Mitchell. *American Science and Invention: A Pictorial History.* New York: Simon & Schuster, 1954.

Winn, Chris, and Jeremy Beadle. *Outlawed Inventions.* Boston: Little, Brown & Company, 1982.

Wulffson, Don L. *Extraordinary Stories Behind the Inventions of Ordinary Things.* New York: Lothrop, Lee & Shepard, 1981.

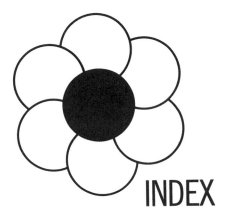

INDEX

Page numbers in *italics*
refer to illustrations.